Chapter One

Get on your bike

BMX Riding Skills

BMX Riding Skills
THE GUIDE TO FLATLAND TRICKS

SHEK HON

FIREFLY BOOKS

A FIREFLY BOOK

Published by Firefly Books Ltd. 2010

First printing

Publisher Cataloging-in-Publication Data (U.S.)

Hon, Shek.
    BMX riding skills : the guide to flatland tricks / Shek Hon.
[122] p. : col. photos. ;   cm.
Includes index.
Summary: A step-by-step guide to BMX bike flatland tricks.
ISBN-13: 978-1-55407-400-6 (pbk.)
ISBN-10: 1-55407-400-2 (pbk.)
1. BMX bikes. I. Title.
629.227/2 dc22   TL437.5B58H65   2010

Library and Archives Canada Cataloguing in Publication

Hon, Shek, 1974-
    BMX riding skills : the guide to flatland tricks / Shek Hon.
Includes index.
ISBN-13: 978-1-55407-400-6
ISBN-10: 1-55407-400-2
    1. BMX bikes. 2. Stunt cycling. 3. Bicycle motocross. I. Title.
GV1049.3.H66 2009   796.6   C2009-905098-6

Published in the United States by
Firefly Books (U.S.) Inc.
P.O. Box 1338, Ellicott Station
Buffalo, New York 14205

Published in Canada by
Firefly Books Ltd.
66 Leek Crescent
Richmond Hill, Ontario L4B 1H1

Conceived and created by
Axis Publishing Limited
www.axispublishing.co.uk

Printed in UAE

BMX riding is an activity with a danger of personal injury, particularly if engaged in without proper safety gear. Participants in this activity should be aware of and accept these risks and accept responsibility for their own actions. Always use good judgment based on a realistic assessment of your own skills and limitations.

Contents

Introduction

Flatland BMX, the art of riding and performing tricks on the flat, is a worldwide phenomenon. You can see it on the streets where you live, in local parks, on the web, and on the worldwide stage in international competitions.

Challenging, infuriating, rewarding, and always absorbing, flatland BMX is addictive. Ask riders what flatland means to them, and you will get a range of answers: the challenge, the countless possibilities, the buzz of accomplishment, the opportunity to express your own style, the chance to deliver like-minded individuals into your friendship group.

If you make it onto the international circuit, flatland can be a way of life. For the leading riders in the world, flatland means high level competition, pushing boundaries, and the chance to share ideas with other ground-breakers.

If you are new to flatland, this book is a good place to start. It shows you exactly how to do the key tricks, and introduces the terms you will come across throughout the genre. If you already enjoy your riding, and want to learn some new moves, you will also find ideas here. Some of the most challenging tricks in the sport are also included, with teaching points to help you break them down into manageable stages.

Everything in this book, from the bike knowledge, history of the sport, to the advanced tricks is included with one aim; to help you become a great flatland rider.

Since the introduction of BMX in the early 70s it has become a worldwide phenomenon. From the Extreme games to its recent introduction into the Olympics, BMX has become arguably one of the most exciting forms of cycling. But before we go into any detail about equipment, or how to perform any tricks, we want you to see what is out there, so you can be inspired to take your riding to a new level. We will outline a brief history, and introduce you to the various disciplines of BMX, racing, street, vert and of course, flatland.

In the beginning

In the early days, kids tried to mimic their motorcycle heroes by riding their cycles on dirt tracks. This Californian craze during the late 1960s ignited a sequence of events that led to the creation of BMX.

The Schwinn Stingray was released in 1963. It was a very successful, mass-produced bicycle that sported small wheels. Although these bicycles had weak frames, with crude geometry, it did not deter riders from emulating their motocross heroes. This became the blueprint for modern BMX, and this evolution has been very well documented in a movie entitled *Joe Kid on a Stingray The History of BMX*.

THE FIRST RACES

Organized dirt bicycle races first appeared in California in 1969, at Santa Monica's Palms Park, organized by Ron Mackler. Longbeach teenager Scot Breithaupt organized races at his local track "Bums." He was one of the early pioneers of BMX, and went on to create SE Bicycles, one of the largest BMX brands to date.

A motocycle film documentary called *On Any Sunday* was released in 1971. The opening sequence featured a bunch of kids racing around a dirt track. Although the sequence only lasted a few minutes, the influence of these scenes played a huge part in inspiring some of the key figures in the development of BMX.

DEVELOPMENT OF THE BIKE

Motocycle companies such as Yamaha started to make motorbike-style bicycles with suspension and mudguards. At the same time, modifications were appearing on Schwinn Stingrays. Straight tubes replaced curved tubes, cranks were extended for greater leverage, and designs increased the bottom bracket height for pedal clearance. These crucial changes were a big step in improving bicycle handling, and a fundamental move to the construction of the bike we know today.

BMX GETS RECOGNIZED

The spread of organized BMX races across America was aided by Ernie Alexander who started the the NBA (National Bicycle Association), the first BMX national sanctioning body in 1974. Bicycle Motocross News, the first national BMX newspaper (published by Elaine Holt), started in the same year. As well as these two major developments, Lin Kastan designed the first manufactured BMX component in 1974 at Red Line Engineering. The Red Line tubular chromoly BMX fork was superior in strength to any previous fork and was a huge hit. Within a few years, Red Line Engineering specialized in BMX manufacture. The basic principle behind the fork design remained unchanged for many years. The first manufactured BMX part was followed by the first frame; a straight-tubed, hard-back, non-suspension frame, manufactured by a company called Webco.

In 1976 Bob Osborn, race starter and photographer, started BMX Action, arguably the most influential BMX magazine ever published. The exceptional photography, and unrivaled passion and energy of the publication spread BMX to a global audience. Other BMX sanctioning groups appeared and BMX spread fast. Huge BMX races such as the Yamaha Gold Cup attracted thousands of spectators, and Steven Spielberg's blockbuster film *ET* was released in 1982 featuring the iconic BMX riding scene. The sport became a multi-million dollar industry.

FREESTYLE

In the late 70s, kids rode their bikes away from their dirt origins to drained-out swimming pools and skateparks. Skateparks introduced designated bike nights. Pioneer Bob Haro demonstrated the rock walk trick in BMX Action magazine, and the BMX Action trick team toured America. Race promoters and bicycle stores realized the popularity of BMX shows, and put on more events. Knowledge of what was to become known as "freestyle" spread.

In 1983 Bob Haro released his first freestyle-specific frameset, designed specifically for trick use, called the "Haro Freestyler." Manufacture snowballed, with every manufacturer releasing freestyle bikes and components. Freestyle BMX became as big as racing.

THE DARK YEARS

After the 80s boom, BMX returned to the underground. Attention had moved to the new money spinner, mountain biking. While the industry was slowing, the riding was definitely not. Riders continue to push the sport to new levels. Mat Hoffman slid rails on bike pegs, and aired 40 ft off the ground with purpose-built 20 ft ramps! Flatland reached new levels with moves like the hitchhiker, invented by Kevin Jones. Rider-run events like the Bicycle Stunts Series were organized by Mat Hoffman. Companies such as Hoffman, Standard and S&M were created by riders and have grown rapidly in popularity. The industry has returned to the hands of the people who loved it most — the riders.

BMX disciplines

From dirt, to street, to skatepark, to flatland, BMX is undoubtedly the most versatile bicycle ever invented. BMX became two main groups: racing and freestyle.

FREESTYLE

Originally freestyle was based on ramps and flatland. Over time this has extended into street and skateparks, and ramps have become more diverse moving from quarter pipes and kickturn ramps, to half pipes, mini ramps, spine ramps and launch ramps. Trails now bridge the gap between racing and freestyle, so where do the boundaries lie? In this section we'll explain the different categories.

RACING

Racing was the first organized discipline of BMX and the popularity has risen with its inception into the Beijing Olympics in 2008. Racing usually consists of 12 BMX riders all competing to be first across the finishing line. The racetrack features including berms, speed jumps, doubles and quadruples. Racing is seen as one of the most competitive forms of BMX, with professional racers enduring extreme training schedules to attain their peak physical fitness.

VERT

Vert riding is half pipe ramp-riding (a U-shaped ramp with sides which reach vertical). These started to appear around the mid- to late-80s; previously riders pedaled across the floor from one quarter pipe to another, until half pipes were brought in to popularity

ABOVE BMX racing is now an Olympic event.

ABOVE Park riding with obstacles such as quarter pipes.

LEFT Flatland riding is performed on flat surfaces, and tricks rely on the rider's skill alone.

BELOW LEFT Dirt jumping over specially designed, and hand-dug trails; one of the earliest forms of BMX riding.

by "2-hip" contest organizer Ron Wilkerson. The advantage of half pipes was the elimination of energy waste caused by pedaling across a flat floor; instead you can pump the ramp.

STREET
Street riding has always existed as riders use the environment around them, from jumping the curb to riding off a loading dock. Always on the quest for new ledges to grind, walls to ride, drops to launch and gaps to clear, street riding in recent years has pushed the limits of what was previously thought possible.

PARK
Skateparks are purpose-built riding environments which can encompass a variety of obstacles such as spine ramps, mini ramps, halfpipes, hips, grind boxes, jump boxes and foam pits. They can be made from concrete, metal or wood.

DIRT JUMPING
One of the earliest forms of riding, dirt jumping started as a side show at BMX races, requiring jumps over table tops or doubles. The jumps grew closer over time and pedaling between jumps became unnecessary. Trails riders invest a great deal of their time digging. The craftsmanship involved with building and maintaining a set of trails is an art form in itself.

Flatland

Some may argue that this discipline is the purest form of BMX, as it is done without the aid of any ramps, tracks or jumps. It encompasses all of the maneuvers done with just you, a BMX and the floor. Beautiful links and unbelievable combinations combine the greatest difficulty, style and creativity.

WHAT MAKES A GOOD RIDER?

One of the first internationally respected flatland riders was Kevin Jones (born 1967). He was innovative with new tricks and positions, and is credited with inventing many of the flatland tricks we know today. He linked tricks together with creativity, flow and style. He gave every sequence of moves an appealing pace and tempo; some were simple, others complicated, but the links and sequences all had a natural ingenuity which was to be copied on a global scale through the "Dorkin" videos made by his friend, Mark Eaton (who was also an incredible flatland rider).

Chase Gouin was next to arrive on the Dorkin scene. His contribution to flatland was an insane level of complexity linking an uncountable number of tricks in sequence. Some of the tricks were uncannily difficult and to this day remain unbeaten. Kevin and Chase are still riding and are very highly respected in the flatland community for their contributions toward riding.

SPONSORSHIP

Get right to the top and sponsorship looks like the ultimate dream, with free bike parts, trainers, clothes, flights around the world and being paid to do what you love. But is it all it's cracked up to be?

The most widespread form of sponsorship is on a local level, with sponsors such as bike shops; being sponsored by a local, independent brand could be a stepping stone on to the sponsorship ladder. With free

equipment, but no payment, local sponsorship is usually referred to as "flow sponsorship." Pro-sponsorship can mean anything from free equipment and travel expenses to a good salary. Top professionals can also earn fees for endorsing and being photographed with their sponsors' product. Unfortunately, the number of pros successfully making a good living out of BMX are few and far between, and any sponsored rider will tell you about the hard work involved.

HOW DO I GET SPONSORED?

Getting sponsored isn't easy, and only a small percentage of riders achieve it; being exceptionally talented isn't always enough. Working hard to consistently place well in contests, and performing well in jams is a good start. Sponsors usually look for an association with your riding talent, your presentation, your look and your style. It might sound obvious but charisma is important, as are approachability, and good people and communication skills. If you appear difficult it can be a real negative, as sponsors rely on their professional riders to set a good example for the fans.

EVENTS

Events are a great place to meet other riders, see current riding trends and see how tricks are done. BMX contests are the perfect place to check out pro-level riding. If you want to pick up tips, check out bikes and get inspired, head toward events. Your local skate park, racetrack or bike shop will be able to put you in touch with forthcoming events. International level flatland contests include King Ground in Japan, Ninja Spin in France, and Level Vibes in the UK. The Redbull "Circle of Balance" was organized one year in a huge, disused gas cylinder; who knows what will be next.

Chapter Two
Getting started

The technological advances on the materials and construction of BMX bicycles have developed a lot in the last 20 years. Here is all the information you need to know to select the bike that suits you, and for you to understand how to get peak performance from it. We show you what to look for in the frame, wheels and pegs. Finally we cover clothing and safety gear. We will also show you the key basic skills to help you get the most from your bike.

Bike anatomy

The BMX bicycle has evolved into a variety of different set-ups in the last 30 years, but there are a number of common elements to all styles.

BMX forks are usually attached with an "A-headset" (see glossary), with a clamp-on stem. Cranks come as three-piece, although some complete bikes are built with a one-piece crank. The various set-ups are usually determined by the style of riding the bike has been designed for. Some bikes, for instance, will only be built with a front brake to allow the forks to spin freely through 360° without the need for a detangler (prevents the rear brake cable from winding itself around the headset). Some flatland riders prefer to have no brakes at all, but this means you have to possess superb bike control and balance. Below is an example of a professional flatland bike.

BELOW Flatland bike, with high-pressure tires, lightweight brake lever, and zero rake position front wheel.

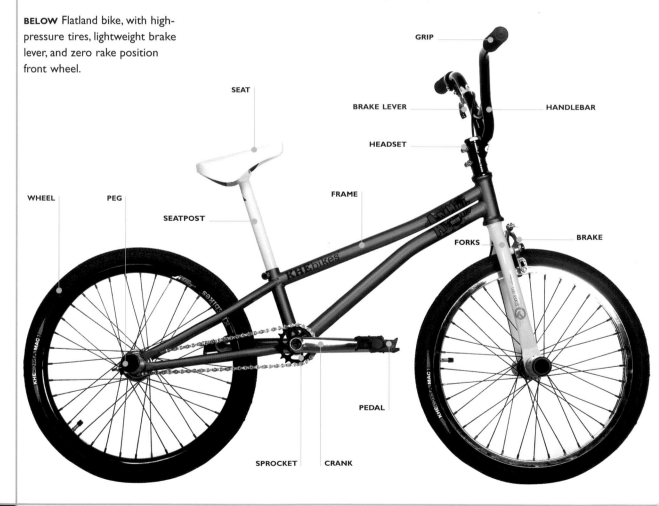

SEAT

GRIP

BRAKE LEVER

HANDLEBAR

HEADSET

WHEEL PEG

FRAME

SEATPOST

FORKS

BRAKE

PEDAL

SPROCKET CRANK

LEFT Most BMX bikes consist of a standard double diamond frame, that is, a frame constructed out of two triangles using 4130 chromoly steel.

BIKE COMPONENTS

HANDLEBARS AND GRIPS

Usually a bike has a handlebar stem, and a handlebar, allowing you to adjust the angle of the handlebars. The bike (shown left) has a fixed position clamp on stem-handlebar combination designed to save weight. The rubber grips are important as they are the contact points between you and your bike.

BRAKE LEVER

A good lightweight lever, with an adjuster for modyifing brake sensitivity.

BRAKE CABLE

A linear slick cable has great flexibility for bending around corners and forks. Try to run the right length cable for optimum braking performance.

HEADSET

The bearing set which enables the steering movement. This headset is referred to as internal, as it features internal cups built into the frame.

FORKS

These forks feature U brake lugs for using using AD brakes. The front wheel is perfectly in the centre of the forks, this is referred to as "zero rake" or "non offset" and is designed for quick response and bar flip tricks.

CRANKS

These are three-piece cranks, named so because they consist of three pieces, two crank arms, and a central spindle. Traditionally stronger and more expensive than one-piece cranks. Flatland bikes usually feature shorter arms (under 175mm) for greater clearance. The cranks on the bike featured, left, boast a luxurious titanium axle which reduces weight but is a very costly option.

BOTTOM BRACKET

Sometimes referred to as a BB, this is the bearing set which holds the cranks to the frame.

PEDALS

These are plastic platform pedals which are less durable than metal, but are good for flatland as they are generally lighter and less sharp.

WHEELS

Wheels come with 48 or 36 spokes and consist of three main components: rims, spokes and hubs. The pattern of spokes has a few different styles: four-cross, three-cross or radial lace.

SPROCKET

Also known as the chainring. Flatland riders prefer small sprockets, giving a lower gearing, making ride outs much easier, and also allows for better clearance.

Hubs, pegs and spokes

Due to the extreme loads put on certain components of a BMX bike, the hubs, pegs and spokes are continually being developed and strengthened for longer durability and reliability.

HUBS

The freecoaster BMX hub enables the bike to roll backward without the pedals moving backward, which is key to many BMX tricks. A regular bicycle rolling backward with a freewheel or cassette hub will rotate the cranks. This is an annoying action as moving cranks get in the way. Most flatland bikes are equipped with a freecoaster hub built into the back wheel. A mechanism inside the hub acts like a clutch to eliminate the rotation through the wheel and keeps cranks in the same position when you are riding. The majority of flatlanders prefer this type of hub, though most professional street, vert, park and dirt riders do not use them.

A cassette hub features an internal paw system mechanism. It uses more internal sealed bearings and relies on a machined piece of aluminum for the freewheel, making the whole hub much sturdier. Cassette hubs are usually slightly more expensive, but benefit from a smoother and stronger type of technology. These hubs also enable smaller sprocket sizes as the freewheels range from eight to thirteen teeth.

PEGS

Riders stand on or hold pegs during tricks. Alloy pegs are the flatlanders' choice; these are typically 4 inches long, and 2 inches wide.

Plastic pegs have occasionally been used in flatland riding but are less durable than alloy/rubber combinations, which remain the choice of most rider's. There are a couple of riders who use steel pegs for flatland, but steel pegs are heavier, slightly slimmer and designed primarily for street use, as the durability of steel is more suitable for grinds.

SPOKES

Spokes are used to hold your wheel together. They come in a variety of different materials, with titanium being the lightest and most expensive. Sometimes spokes are double-butted which means they differ in thickness from one end to another, saving crucial bits of weight on a wheel.

LEFT This bike features pegs on the front wheel. Alloy pegs are first choice for most flatland riders.

RIGHT Pegs in use during this trick. They need to be strong enough to take your entire weight.

Clothing and shoes

Finding the right clothes for flatland is largely dependent on personal choice. It sounds obvious but, better fitting clothes are less likely to get caught on bike parts, and allow better flexibility during tricks.

Riders like to go for flatland associated brands like Stereo Panda or Emer clothing which have been created and endorsed by flatland riders. It's a positive move to support brands which support BMX. Orchid and Lotek are shoe brands run by BMX riders and design their shoes with BMX riding in mind, featuring good durability, padding and grippy rubber soles.

Other brands who have invested interest in BMX include brands such as Etnies, DC and Vans who all also boast terrific BMX teams. When choosing a shoe for flatland, a good, comfortable fit and durable grip is essential, and comes in extra handy for any type of scuffing trick. Padding and ankle protection is important, too, but get a good balance of padding and flexibility.

PROTECTIVE EQUIPMENT

When you are learning new tricks for the first time, it is a good idea to wear protective gear. Many of the professionals you see in the magazines have been riding for many years, and have developed experience and skills to limit their injuries. When you are starting out it is a good idea to attempt tricks that are within your capabilities, and even then I can guarantee you will fall off the bike, so I recommend you wear protective equipment including crash helmets, gloves, and knee, elbow and shin pads.

GLOVES
Shown here are full finger gloves, but for a little more control over the brakes you could use fingerless gloves.

SHIN PADS
Shins are another part of your anatomy that will be regularly bashed by cranks, handlebars and the frame. Choose a well-padded set of guards to keep you riding longer.

HELMET
There are a variety of helmet brands on the market, all offering slightly different takes on the classic design. Things to look out for are: good-quality padding on the inside; a strap system that allows you to get a tight but not restrictive fit; and air holes at the top to allow heat and sweat to escape.

ANKLE PADS
Ankles are particularly prone to knocks, so a good pair of ankle pads are essential.

Basic bike skills

Before trying to master any of the tricks in this book, take time to familiarize yourself with how your bike handles. Practice standing on the rear pegs, and rolling along standing. Also practice stepping back onto the pedals.

When riding flatland there are a couple of general tips you should try to stick to. Before you attempt a trick, visualize the trick from start to end, and think about the positioning of your arms and legs. Which direction will you be facing? Try to be aware of the space around you, and visualize where your body is relative to the ground. With many flatlands tricks your body should be upright, with your head facing slightly lower than parallel to the floor. There are exceptions, but this is a good starting point.

BAILS AND DABS

Plan how to bail out of your tricks before you attempt them; if you can jump out of tricks like a cat you can limit the extent of your crashes. If you are new to a trick, try to keep regular contact with the floor with at least one foot until it feels comfortable. This is known as "dabbing" and it is essential during practice. Keep regular contact with the floor with one foot pushing along to find your balance point.

REAR PEGS

Establish a comfortable, smooth riding speed on the pedals with your body weight forward.

Move your right foot to the rear peg smoothly, and maintain your speed.

Now move your left foot to the rear peg smoothly, and maintain your speed and balance.

BREAKING A TRICK DOWN

Many tricks require practice and patience; professional riders practice for hours every day. Try a variety of ways to practice; sometimes you need to run through the trick repeatedly before you can perfect it, but there are times when it is better to break the trick down into small stages and attempt a stage at a time. If you are stuck on a certain trick, tackle the second half rather than the first; this can give you more confidence and build your skill base. Practice the middle or end part of a trick an equal number of times as the first part.

FLOOR

Try to find a flat surface for practice. Uneven paving slabs, cracks and bumps can put off the most experienced rider. Indoor spots are ideal for flatland riders as they are free from the weather, and tend to be smoother. Slight inclines can be handy for help with rolling tricks.

FRONT AND REAR PEGS

Move your right foot back to the pedal, then your left, maintaining your speed. Prepare to lift your left foot.

Place your left foot on the right rear peg, transfer your weight to your left foot keep your speed and balance constant.

Step forward with your right foot to your front right peg. Try to maintain your balance, before returning to the pedals.

Chapter Three

Tricks for beginners

So, you've seen a bit of flatland and you want to give it a go? This section takes you through some of the classic moves step-by-step. We'll guide you through the basic introductory tricks that every rider needs to master, from the classic wheelie to your first rolling trick. We will then introduce you to new balance points and different positions in order to familiarize you with your bike and get you ready for the more demanding tricks.

Now, your bike is ready, and you are geared up for the riding — enjoy your entry into the world of flatland!

Endo

The endo is a useful basic move, and the starting point for many more advanced tricks. You can start by lifting the back wheel as low as you like, and as you get more confident and feel more balanced, raise the wheel as high as you dare. This is a trick you will always come back to, so it is worth taking the time now to perfect it.

Roll along with the pedals level. Keep an even speed, and try to move steadily, but slowly to begin with.

Pull the front brake hard, and at the same time, push forward on the handlebars and lean forward. Your back wheel will start to lift.

Compress your knees and bend your legs. Lean as far forward as you can while keeping your body weight centered over the bike. Your arms should be straight and strong.

As you start to reach the maximum peak before you feel like you are going to tip over forward, tuck your body over the back wheel as far as you can to balance the bike.

Allow the back wheel to drop back toward the ground, and release the brake. Keep your balance as your wheels return to the ground.

Start pedaling hard to keep your forward momentum and balance, and move forward with your weight balanced evenly over the bike.

Back hops

Back hops are a good basic skill to help beginners learn bike control by exploring its balance. They are also the foundation for tricks such as wheelies and manuals or tire taps on ramps. However hopping is not good practice when actually performing a trick. This basic trick can form the start of any practice session, even as you become more experienced.

Roll forward slowly, standing up with the pedals level. Keep your balance, with your weight centered over the bike. Try to keep a slow, but steady speed.

Pull a small endo, so your back wheel lifts off the ground. Keep the handlebars straight, and check your balance.

Pull the back brake, and lean back. When the back wheel touches the ground, pull on the handlebars and lift the front wheel off the ground.

Balance on the back wheel, and take a moment to check that your body is centered over the bike and you feel stable. Start hopping; try small hops to start with just to get a feel for the trick.

Hop on the spot, and aim to increase the height of your hop. If you feel as though your balance needs correcting, hop toward the direction you are falling toward. For example, if you feel you are falling to the left, hop left.

When you have finished hopping, drop the front wheel and release the brake. Start pedaling to move into your next trick.

Bunnyhops

The bunnyhop is the building block for a huge variety of different maneuvers. It's a great way of teaching yourself how to control the bike while in your natural riding position. Bunnyhops are useful tricks to master as they enable you to hop onto obstacles, off steps and into different grinds.

Ride along at a comfortable speed, and then stand up with your pedals level. Keep your balance, with your weight centered over the bike.

Crouch down over your bike, by compressing your body. Bend your arms and legs, and keep your back straight. Pedal if you need to to keep your speed constant.

Spring up by straightening your legs and arms. At the same time, pull back and upward on the handlebars to lift the front wheel off the ground and into a wheelie position.

As the front wheel lifts off the ground, bend your legs and bring the bike into you as close as possible, lifting the back wheel off the ground. Keep your core strong, and your arms straight and strong.

When you land, bend your arms and legs like springs to absorb the shock of the landing. Keep your core strong to protect your back.

Aim to land both wheels on the ground as gently as possible. Check that your wheels are aligned before you cycle off.

Barspin (ground)

This is the classic 360 degree barspin, and it forms the basis of the bunnyhop bar spin. Master this trick on the ground first, to get an idea of the dynamics of the trick.

Ride along slowly, with your weight centered over the bike. Get a reasonable speed on the bike, and a firm grip on the handlebars.

Start to pull back so the front wheel comes off the floor. Squeeze the seat with your knees so you have a tight grip on your bike. Your legs and arms should be straight, with your weight toward the back.

Start to rotate your handlebars in a clockwise direction. This has to be a quick move; you throw the bars into the rotation. Balance so your front wheel stays off the floor for enough time for the bars to go around. Lean back enough for the front wheel to leave the floor, but not so much you fall off the back.

TIP
You can break this down by trying a half barspin, where the handlebars rotate through 180 degrees. When you are comfortable with this, progress to practicing the full 360 degree barspin.

When the handlebars reach 270 degrees, place your catching hand in front of you, to catch the handlebars as they come round. Keep your legs strong and straight, with control over the pedals, and continue to grip the bike seat with your thighs.

Shift your weight forward and catch one grip, quickly followed by catching the other grip. Make sure your knees continue to grip the bike seat.

Shift your weight upward, and release your grip on the seat. Let the front wheel drop down gently. Balance your feet on the pedals, and start pedaling to move forward.

Front hops

A great old school basic, front hops demonstrate that you have control over your bike, but are frowned upon unless used to connect tricks such as barspins, crankflips and tailwhips. They are also the foundations for nose wheelies and mini ramp tricks such as nosepicks (a front wheel stall on a mini ramp deck).

Cruise along with the pedals level. This move starts in an endo position, so pull the front brake, and get into your endo position. Check that your balance is strong, and your weight is centered over the bike.

Lean forward and place your body weight on your arms as well as your legs. Check that you feel balanced.

Lift the back wheel as high as you dare, and start hopping. When you first try this trick, start with small hops just to get a feel for the trick. Bend your arms and knees to soften the impact as you hop.

Hop on the spot and just like back hops, correct your position if your balance needs adjustment, by moving toward the direction you feel you are tipping toward.

Try a variety of positions and hopping in different directions. Aim to lift your back wheel as high as you can, while maintaining control of the bike. Keep your core strong.

When you have finished hopping, drop the back wheel, release the brake and check that your balance is centered. Start pedaling.

Wheelie

The wheelie is one of the most famous BMX tricks, and you will see it performed by experienced BMXers and stunt motorcyclists. Once mastered, you can try variations, such as traveling along while pedaling for whichever distance you choose, or simply cruising in the position without pedaling.

Travel along at a comfortable speed, with your weight centered over the bike. Stand in the pedals, with your arms strong and straight.

Pull back at the same time as pedaling, so your weight shifts to the back of the bike. You can do this either when standing up or sitting down. Keep your arms straight and continue to pedal.

As the front wheel starts to lift, transfer your weight back so you feel in control. Maintain an upright posture and do not hunch over the handlebars.

Control how high the front wheel rises by the speed of your pedaling. The faster you pedal, the higher the front wheel will lift. To control and lower the front wheel, slow down the pedaling.

Move your knees to either side to control and correct your balance. Find a 50/50 balance between the speed of pedaling and the amount of back brake you use.

To complete the move, lean forward and gently squeeze the back brake to allow the front wheel to drop slowly back to the ground. Check that your wheels are aligned on contact to maintain control of the bike.

Rockwalk

The classic rockwalk is the art of pivoting your bike through 180 degree rotations with the brakes on. You perform it on both wheels in turn, with the front one the usual wheel to turn first, so you complete a 360 degree circle. Done smoothly, it looks like your bike is "walking."

Roll along at a moderate speed, with your weight evenly placed over the bike. Before you start, visualize rotating 180 degrees on the front wheel so your mind is engaged.

Pull the front brake, and lean forward. Twist your body around and pivot 180 degrees on your front wheel. Bring the back wheel around cleanly, and at an even speed. Turn your head in the direction that you are turning so you can see where you are going, and your body moves in the direction you need to go.

As you complete your 180 degree pivot on the front wheel, pull on the back brake. Bring your weight smoothly back to the center of the bike.

TIP
You can repeat this walk many times to create the illusion of the bike walking. Rotate backward then forward again. You will need to build more speed for more continuous rotations.

As your back wheel drops and touches the floor, continue your rotation another 180 degrees, but this time on your back wheel. Lean backward so your weight is over the back wheel, and the front wheel lifts.

As you complete the turn, bring your weight to the center of your bike. Keep your core strong and the front lifted until you are completely around.

When you are facing forward again, release the brakes and let the front wheel touch the ground. Start pedaling to move forward, or move into another rockwalk.

Peg wheelie

A beautiful, straightforward rolling trick, where you do a wheelie while standing on a rear stunt peg. Aim to be able to perform this trick on both sides of the bike. To balance, swing your free leg forward and back as a counter-balance.

Coast along with one foot and both hands on the handlebars at a comfortable speed. This trick works best if you are going fast enough, but don't go faster than you are comfortable with.

Lean back, and swing your left leg back to stand on your left wheel peg. Keep your arms strong, and your balance centered over the bike.

Pull with your arms to pick up your front wheel. Lift your right leg away from your pedal and swing it back as a counter-balance. Look forward and try and keep straight, using your right leg for balance. Put your fingers over the brake, as a safety measure; if you fall too far backward, pull the brake.

Swing your leg back and forth to maintain balance. You can try to lean from side to side to help keep the bike in a straight line. Keep your arms straight and your swinging leg relaxed. Aim to lift the handlebar up until almost vertical.

Lean forward, place the front wheel back on the floor and your foot back on the pedals. Aim to put your wheel down gently, rather than slamming it to the ground.

Shift your body weight back, and check that both wheels are aligned before you cycle away.

Rollback

Sometimes known as a "fakie," a roll back is essentially rolling backward while in your riding position. You can attempt this by bunny hopping into it, or rolling backward with the aid of a ramp, or endo-ing into it, which we show here.

To practice a roll back, you can start off the same way as a rockwalk, with a 180 degree endo. Establish a good speed, with your weight balanced over your bike.

Pivot around on your front wheel, with you standing. Adjust your body position so you face the direction of rotation. Rotate 180 degrees; it can help to visualize this as you do it.

Look in the direction you are traveling. This helps to move your shoulders and body round. Swing the back of your bike round to complete the entire rotation.

TIP
You can do roll backs either sitting on
the seat or standing up, as shown here.
Neither is easy!

When your bike has completed the rotation, land your back wheel so you and the bike are facing the way you came. Try and keep upright, with your weight centered over the bike. Pedal backward to counteract the freewheel moving. You can use your handlebars to steer, making minor adjustments to keep yourself upright.

Try to keep yourself in a straight line by keeping your body weight centralized. Aim for two or three back pedals.

Pull out of the trick as you would a rockwalk: pull the back brake and rotate round bringing your front wheel facing forward. Look in the direction that you are rotating. Land the front wheel gently, and make sure your wheels are aligned before moving forward.

Cyclone

This is one of the first tricks many flatland riders learn. You roll along backward standing on the front peg and twist around to get back on your bike. This is a useful trick as there are many moves and links which put you in this backward position, and learning the cyclone is a good way of getting you back on the pedals facing the right way.

Roll along at a comfortable speed with your hands on the grips, left foot on the rear peg and the right foot on the front peg.

Push off from the rear peg and rotate 180 degrees standing with your right foot on the front peg, dab the brakes if you feel more comfortable.

Your body should be facing backward and the rest of bike should remain in the original direction. Roll backward with one foot on the front peg and the other foot on the rear peg. Making minor adjustments to your steering to keep balance.

When you are ready, pivot your front foot on the peg, turning your head to face forward again and rotate around 180 degrees.

Place your front foot back on the pedal and get ready to cycle off.

If you have trouble with the rotation, you have an option of keeping your arms crossed over until you are facing forward again, or rotating all in one motion.

Squeaker

This trick is an introduction into some true flatland tricks, and the first scuffing trick of the book. Scuffing is where you use your foot to move the wheel, and is an art in itself. The combination of kicking the front tire backward and feathering (lightly applying) the brakes for balance leads to a squeaking sound. The squeaker move is a great foundation for learning bike control with your feet.

Roll along slowly with your right foot on the pedal and your left foot on the front peg. Your body should be centered between the two.

Pull the front brake so your back wheel lifts off the floor. As the rear wheel lifts off the floor, put your right foot on the front tire.

When you feel balanced and comfortable, scuff the tire with your foot to go backward. Keep your fingers over the brake as a safety precaution, and pull it if you feel a bit too far forward.

Be careful not to scuff the wheel too much and go over the handlebars. Start off with some small shuffles until you find the right pace.

You should be able to give a consistent shuffle with your foot on the tire to move you into a backward motion while balancing on the front wheel.

When you are ready to complete the move, drop the back wheel gently by pulling the brake. Step back onto the pedals ready to cycle forward again once you have completed the trick.

Switzerland squeaker

The Switzerland squeaker is a variation on the classic squeaker trick, but uses both feet running along the top of the front wheel. It was named by RL Osborn, when he was in Switzerland. The tire is narrow so be careful with running along the top of it.

Start off in the same way as you would for a squeaker. Roll in with one foot on the pedal and one foot on the front peg. Keep your weight evenly balanced over the bike frame.

As the rear wheel lifts off the floor, adjust your balance so your weight comes forward. Keep a tight hold on the grips. Move to put your left foot on the front tire.

When you feel comfortable, scuff the tire with your foot to go backward, followed with a scuff from the other foot imediately. Keep your fingers over the brake as a safety precaution, pulling it if you feel too far forward.

Alternate scuffing the tire with your feet. Be careful not to scuff the wheel too much and go over the handlebars. Start off with some small shuffles until you find the right pace.

Do consistent shuffles with your feet on the tire to move you into a steady backward motion balancing on the front wheel.

When you have completed the move, drop the back wheel by pulling the brake and step back onto the pedals to move away.

Tailwhip

This version of the tailwhip (also known as the footjam tailwhip), is a nice balance trick where you kick your frame around 360 degrees keeping the handlebars stationary. The back end ("tail") of the bike needs to whip around at speed to complete the move cleanly. There are many variations on this trick, so once you have mastered this, you can progress to a variety of moves. You can try kicking the bike with your back foot to give it extra momentum. It is difficult to get your timing correct for this movement, but after a bit of practice the timing will become more natural.

Roll along with you feet standing on the pedals, at a fairly slow, comfortable speed to begin with.

Place your right leg over the top tube of the bike so it is to one side of your bike. Rest your foot just under the tube while you steady your balance.

Place your right foot onto the front tire, and stand firmly on it. Pull the front brake and at the same time, kick the back of your bike around with your left foot.

While the back of the bike is traveling round, move your handlebars in a circular direction and try to keep your head up. You need to control the handlebars so that the back wheel stays in mid-air. Use your free foot as balance, moving it to act as a counterbalance to the swinging bike frame.

When the frame completes the rotation, catch the top of the frame with your free foot. Straighten the handlebars so they are in line with the frame.

Place your free foot back on its pedal, then the one from the wheel. Steady the bike and get into position to move forward at the end of the trick.

Boomerang

In this trick, you put your weight on the handlebars to jump and rotate yourself 360 degrees over the front of your bike, before landing back on your bike. You can do this trick from the back stunt peg, from the frame or from the pedals. This example demonstrates doing a boomerang from the rear pegs.

Roll along slowly with one foot on the rear peg, and with both hands on the handlebars.

Jump off the rear peg and put your weight onto your handlebars, you then spin round on the handlebars 360 degrees — feather your front brake as a safety precaution.

Tuck your legs in tight to your body, and spin around while you turn the handlebars 360 degrees. Keep your legs lifted, and lean forward. Be careful not to lean too far forward as you could risk going over the handlebars; if you feel your weight falling forward, kick your legs back to bring your weight backward.

As your handlebars pass the halfway point, start to unfold your legs ready to get back on the pedals or pegs.

Place your closest foot back on to the frame. As you progress, you could try to put your first landing foot back on to the rear peg.

Land facing forward and place your other foot back on the pedal or peg as soon as you can. Once you are comfortably back in position, check that your wheels are aligned, once complete, ride off.

Intermediate tricks

By now you will have mastered some of the basic maneuvers and you are interested in taking your riding to the next level. The tricks in this section are guaranteed to impress even the strictest of critics.

We move on to a collection of impressive scuffing tricks, as well as impressive front wheel moves such as the front yard and side squeaks. You will learn fast spinning tricks such as the megaspin. We also include the most popular and incredibly versatile rolling trick, the steamroller.

Spinning peg wheelie

This is a variation on a peg wheelie, designed to enable you to move in circles; you use the back wheel as your pivot. It's a great trick that you can use to to link into other tricks, and it's fun to spin fast in tight circles. As you progress you can work your bike round in figure eight maneuvers.

Establish a steady speed, with your balance evenly distributed over the bike. Stand on your back wheel pegs, with your legs straight.

Carve in an arc and start to pull into a peg wheelie by leaning back. At the same time, pull with your arms to pick up your front wheel. Swing one leg back ready to balance.

Using your free leg for balance, rotate the bike away from the peg you are standing on. Your balancing foot has a slightly different position in a circular peg wheelie and you can leave it more outward than a regular peg wheelie.

Control the tightness of your spin by how much you hold yourself in. To spin the peg wheelie in tighter circles pull the front wheel higher and bring your bike closer to your body, and hold your balancing leg closer in.

If you want to slow the rotational speed of the spinning wheelie, position your leg further back and lower your front wheel.

To complete the move, lean forward and place the front wheel back on the floor. At the same time, place your free foot back on the pedal, followed by the foot that was on the rear peg.

Infinity Roll

A good basic backward moving balancing trick. You keep both wheels on the floor, and cruise backward, aiming to maintain an even speed. This is an easy trick to step into, and once you have mastered it, practice to see how long you can keep rolling for.

Cycle forward and establish a steady comfortable speed. As you roll forward, place your feet on the rear pegs. Check that your hands are firm on the handlebars. Get ready to place one foot on the rear tire.

Pull your front brake to do a small endo to get the bike rolling backward. As you roll backward, take your inside foot off the peg and use this for balance. Don't be afraid to dab the floor with this foot if you feel unbalanced. Start to turn the handlebars in the opposite direction you want to rotate.

Continue to turn the handlebars, and when you feel balanced, scuff the rear tire, so you go in a backward motion. Make minor adjustments to your steering to keep your balance.

Check your body position; you need to get your central balance correct so if you scuff the wheel backward, prepare for your weight to fall forward. Make sure you don't have too much weight forward as this may prevent you from steering.

Continue to scuff the rear tire for as long as you are able to hold the trick. Experienced riders are able to trace a specific path with the bike, so aim for a guided path, or a figure eight.

When you are ready to pull out of the trick, pull your rear brake, step back on the pedals and ride off.

Backward steamroller

Now you are ready to get into some real flatland. The steamroller is an absolute essential in flatland riding; it is useful for many different links, and it feels great to perform. It is a versatile trick to roll forward, backward or take you spinning in a circle.

Roll along at a comfortable speed with your hands on the grips. Place one foot on the rear peg and the other foot on the front peg.

Push off from the rear peg and rotate yourself 180 degrees until you are in front of your bike; the handlebars should come around with you. Swing your free leg around alongside you for balance. Your body should be facing backward and the rest of bike should remain pointing in the original direction.

Grab the seat with your hand (use the one on the same side as your standing leg). When you feel comfortable, lean back and pull the seat. Lift the back wheel putting you in the correct position for a backward steamroller. Use your free leg for balance, swinging it back and forth like a pendulum.

Roll backward with one foot on the peg and the foot in the air. The forward motion of the bike should keep you moving backward.

When you have finished, rotate you and the handlebars around 180 degrees. Keep hold of the seat and swing your leg to move you around.

Place your foot back on the frame and then your foot back on the pedal. You can jump into this position if you prefer.

180 bunnyhop

A bunnyhop refers to jumping both the front and back wheel off the ground at the same time. This trick is essentially a bunnyhop with an 180 degree rotation. Some people find it easier to hop over obstacles such as a cardboard box, rather than flat ground. Similar to the regular bunnyhop, you can progress this to street, hopping up curbs or off obstacles.

Roll along at a comfortable speed. Try to visualize the turn before you start; the aim will be to face backward after completing the maneuver.

On the approach, compress your body down, with your knees and arms bent. Then spring up and rotate at the same time by pulling up on the handlebars. Here, the bike is turning to the left.

Lift the back wheel as you continue to rotate to your left (try it to the right another time). Your legs should be strong and straight, and use your core to keep your body strong.

Look in the direction of rotation, for example, when rotating left, look over your left shoulder.

As you get ready to land, be aware that you are going to roll back. Land the back wheel first, and compress your legs as you land to absorb the shock.

Land your front wheel down as gently as possible. Check that the wheels are aligned before moving forward again.

Fire Hydrant

The fire hydrant is a variation of a tailwhip, where you move the bike around you. It is a great trick for combinations, or you can simply do by itself. You can land it onto the frame, onto the peg or use it to link into other tricks such as a decade (see page 74).

Start out rolling quite slowly. Place your inside foot on the rear peg, and your outside foot on the front peg. Aim to keep the speed constant, and the wheels aligned at this point.

Push off with the foot on the front peg, and turn the handlebars around approximately 180 degrees. Hold firm onto the handlebars and stand firm on the front peg.

When the front wheel is facing backward, swing your back leg around so you are standing on both pegs on your front wheel. This will put you facing the back-end of the bike. You may want to overturn to wherever you feel comfortable.

Pull back on the handlebars to lift the rear wheel off the ground. As it lifts up, pull the front brake and lean the handlebars completely to the side so the bike comes around. During this you are standing on one front peg, using your free leg for balance.

As the bike comes around, catch the frame of the bike with your free foot. Bring the wheels back into alignment.

Step your front foot back onto the pedal, make sure the handlebars are aligned, ready to ride away.

Half Cab

This trick is essentially a bunnyhop done backward with a 180 degree turn thrown in too. In many ways the half cab has become a new 180 bunnyhop, and riders use it to hop up or down from obstacles. It is an impressive way to get out of a fakie and takes your skillset to a whole new level.

To begin this trick, start with a 180 degree endo. Your legs should be compressed, as you lift the rear wheel to get some momentum going.

Roll back, and back pedal until the pedals are level. At this point, lock the pedal with your foot to lift the front.

As your front wheel lifts off the floor, turn your head and handlebars to face the direction you want to rotate in (here it is shown to the left). In the early days of mastering this move, you can pivot the first part of the rotation on your back wheel before your bike leaves the floor.

As the bike comes around, compress your body again, with your knees and arms bent. Your handlebars should be in line with the frame, and you are facing back toward the direction in which you started.

As the front wheel lifts, spring upward similar to a bunnyhop and twist your body in the direction you wish to rotate in. Spin the bike around, using the handlebars and your core strength to get you around.

Rotate the bike around and land facing forward. Aim to land the wheels gently. Bend your knees as you land to absorb the shock. Check the frame and wheels are aligned before moving off.

Slider

A slider is a stylish way of getting out of a fakie (rollback). You turn the handlebars through 180 degrees and the bike spins around with both tires in contact with the floor all the way through the trick. The tires basically "slide" through the maneuver, and the aim is to be as smooth as possible.

Set yourself up for a fakie rollback; you can do this either by starting with a 180 degree endo, or a 180 degree bunnyhop.

When you are comfortable, turn your handlebars 180 degrees while still holding on to the grips with your arms crossed (this position is known as an "x-up"). Start to turn the handlebars in the direction you want to rotate. X-up the bars clockwise, if you want to rotate out of the fakie clockwise, and vice versa.

Continue to turn the handlebars, and turn your head to face the direction you want to spin.

Pull your inside grip and steer the bike so the handlebars maintain a straight path. Move the handlebars in a natural movement where you pull them forward in front of you, and make sure there is clearance for the handlebars to get past (keep your knees clear).

The trick with pulling a smooth slider is having your body weight in the correct position: lean back a little to begin with, but experiment with moving your weight forward. Move forward too soon and the bike can spit you over the handlebars, so be careful.

The rear end of the bike should steer to the side and go through a backward to forward direction.

Steamroller

We showed you how to perform the backward steamroller on page 62; this classic steamroller goes forward, and is slightly trickier. The steamroller is one of the most natural, enjoyable rolling tricks because the position is comfortable, with a lot of room to maneuver.

Roll along at a comfortable speed with your hands on the grips. Place your inside foot on the rear wheel peg and the outside foot on the front peg. Continue to roll along at a steady speed.

Turn the handlebars and front wheel so the front wheel is facing the back of the bike. Use the leg on the rear peg to help bring the frame around. Turn your head to face the back of the bike.

As the handlebars go around, use your free leg to balance. You may need to stretch your leg backward to stop yourself from falling over the handlebars. Stand on the front pegs if you like. As the frame reaches the 180 position, grab hold of the seat with your hand.

Use your free leg for balance, swinging it back and forth like a pendulum. Aim to roll along smoothly for as long as you can.

When you wish to get back onto the bike, move the frame past 90 degrees and drop the back wheel on the floor. Drop the seat and aim to place your free balancing foot back on the frame.

Place your other foot back on the pedal and ride off.

Decade

Like many flatlands tricks, there are a number of different ways of performing a decade. You can jump from the frame, or a peg or from another trick. This can be a scary trick to learn so break it down in to stages at first (see box right).

Ride along slowly with your inside foot on the rear peg and your other foot on the front peg.

Keeping your foot on the rear peg (or pedal if you prefer), move one foot onto the top tube of the frame. Keep your pedals level, with the pedal forward on the other side to where your body starts; this makes the trick a lot easier to ride out of.

Pull both brakes to do a slight endo; you want just enough momentum for you to lift the back wheel off the floor. Keep the back wheel just above the ground (no more than 3 inches).

Pull the back brake. When the rear wheel drops you should have enough momentum for the front wheel to rise and for you to pull the bike into a vertical position. It is a good idea when you start learning this trick to pull the wheel up gradually before reaching the vertical position.

As the bike reaches its vertical position, jump over the top of the bike to the other side. Keep your hand firm on the handlebars and pull your knees in close to your body.

As you clear the bike, place one foot on top of the frame. Aim to land the bike gently, with your knees bent to absorb the shock. Place your other foot on the pedal and ride off.

Front yard

As scuffing tricks go, the front yard is one of the more natural tricks to get in and out of. Everything can move in a forward direction, and you should flow forward nicely. If you want to progress this trick, try one-handed, no-handed, circular versions or your own combination.

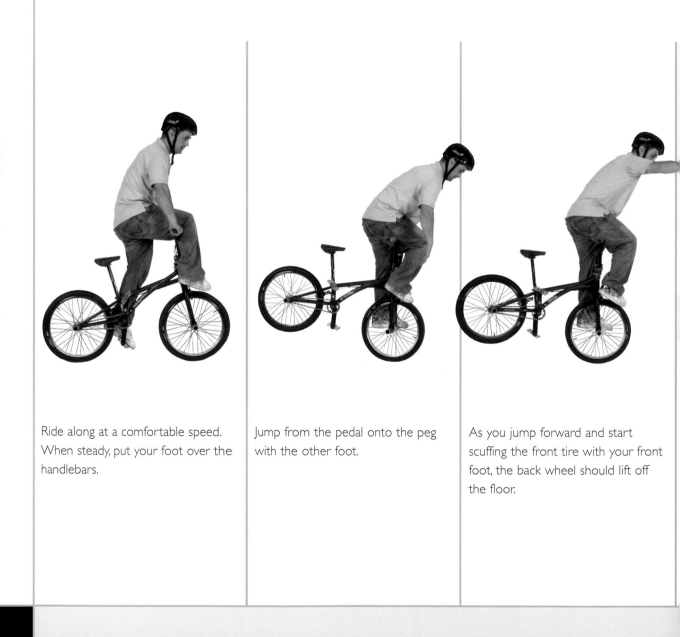

Ride along at a comfortable speed. When steady, put your foot over the handlebars.

Jump from the pedal onto the peg with the other foot.

As you jump forward and start scuffing the front tire with your front foot, the back wheel should lift off the floor.

To control your balance in this position, use your free hand as a counterweight to constantly adjust your body position.

You can also scuff the wheel in the direction that you want to go. Use your whole body on the handlebars to steer the direction of the trick.

When you have finished rolling this trick, drop the rear wheel back on to the floor. Move your foot from the peg onto the pedal and then bring your foot back over the handlebars and onto the other pedal.

Side squeaks

This is a nice, slow, backward scuffing trick. It is one of the safer tricks to learn and useful for linking front wheel tricks. The trick is initially quite difficult to learn, because of its asymmetric positioning.

Ride along slowly with both hands on the handlebars, place one foot on the front peg and one foot on the back peg so you are standing to the side of the bicycle.

Pull the front brake, so the bike endos and the rear wheel lifts off the floor. Grab the seat with your inside hand (the hand closest to the seat).

Place your rear foot on the tire, holding your seat on the side. Have your front hand on the brake for safety.

Scuff gently backward on the tire, and feathering the front brake to help control the trick. Scuff in the direction you want to go. The trick will naturally roll in a circle.

Keep the top half of your body locked with the handlebars. You can move the seat and bike to adjust the weight and balance.

When you are ready to come out of the trick, you have a couple of options: drop the frame and place it in front of you to go into a backward steamroller, or drop the seat and place your scuffing foot back on the back peg, before moving your front foot back onto the pedals.

Funky chicken

This trick is like the front yard, with the bike in front of you instead of behind you. Your foot is over the handlebars and you scuff the tire to move forward, while you balance on your front wheel.

Start off with a backward steamroller position. Roll along at a comfortable speed with your hands on the grips, one foot on the rear peg and the other foot on the front peg.

Push off from the rear peg and rotate your body through 180 degrees until you are facing the back of the bike. Place your leg over the handlebars. Grab the seat with your hand. Keep your legs straight and strong.

Use your foot to control the speed of the tire by scuffing. If you are going too fast, use your foot as a brake. If you feel like your rear wheel is going to drop, speed up your scuffs.

Lift the seat of the bike to add difficulty. Steer the bike by leaning toward the direction you want to go. To begin with it is safer to do short scuffs so you have a good contact with the tire. As you grow more confident, change the pace of your scuffs. Try to look toward the direction you are going.

When you are finished rolling this trick, swing your leg round again until you are over the pedal.

Place the rear wheel back on the floor, let go of the seat and bring your foot back over the handlebars. Place your foot on the frame and ride off.

McCircle

A continuous, backward scuffing steamroller. The aim is to do it in a neat, circular motion. The trick may appear to be very similar to a steamroller, and the balance points are similar, but the actions and the feeling of it are totally unique.

Roll along at a comfortable speed with your hands on the grips. Place your inside foot on the rear peg and the outside foot on the front peg.

Push off from the rear peg and rotate yourself 180 degrees. Your body should be facing backward and the rest of bike should remain in the original direction.

Roll backward with one foot on the peg and the other foot scuffing the tire backward. Lean into the curve so you go in a circular direction.

Use your foot as a brake, to slow yourself down, or scuff at a faster pace to speed yourself up. It is possible to make adjustments to your balance by steering, and to alter the position of your seat or bike with your other hand.

When you have finished, rotate back through 180 degrees.

Place your foot back on the frame, let the rear wheel drop back to the floor and then place your foot back on pedal.

Half lash (smoothie out)

This is also known as a half whiplash. You start the trick in the same way as a steamroller. The example shown here features a switch-foot, with an exit style called a "smoothie."

Roll along at a comfortable speed, with your hands on the grips. Place your inside foot on the front peg this time, and your outside leg on the rear peg. This is like the start of a steamroller but with your feet switched over.

Kick the frame around and move your handlebars in a counter-clockwise motion to help the frame spin around the bike. Use your free leg to help balance you.

Let the rear wheel drop onto the ground, and place your other foot back onto the rear peg or on the bike frame. You may need to stretch backward to stop yourself from falling.

Carve in a circle by steering the handlebars. Keep your legs flexible by bending them to adjust the distance between you and the bike. At this point you can practice bailing out of the trick as many times as you need to, to get to master the balance point.

Scuff the rear tire to keep the bike moving. Use your body as a counter-balance, aiming to keep upright. When you are ready, let the front wheel pass the frame, so the rear part of the bike pivots from a backward to forward motion. This part of the trick is called a smoothie.

Keep your body weight far enough back so you don't fall over the handlebars, but forward enough to stay on the bike. Step back onto the pedals to return to the standard riding position.

Megaspin

This is a backward spinning wheelie. The aim is to make it as smooth and continuous as you can. It is one of the first recommended rear wheel spinning tricks. You can practice it by breaking it down in stages first.

Start off as if you were about to perform a spinning peg wheelie. Do an initial rotation until the rear wheel pivots round. Use your free leg to bring the frame around.

At the pivot point, the wheel will start to spin backward. Place one foot on the rear peg and one on the pedal.

Use your outside foot to start scuffing the tire backward. Lift the front of the bike and find your balance point.

Keep a consistent pumping motion with continuous scuffing to keep the bike going in a circular motion. Initially it will feel like there is a resistance to this spin; the bike will feel like it wants to stop spinning or go forward.

Keep yourself and the bike leaning slightly inward (toward the center) and back. Turn the handlebars as you scuff round.

To pull out of the trick, swing your free leg round until you can place it back on the pedal. Keep the handlebar straight and look forward. Place your front wheel down and ride off. You need to keep scuffing the tire to keep going in a circular direction

Advanced tricks

This section gets into some serious flatland territory. You want to take your riding right to the limits? You want to have the biggest moves? Well, you've come to the right place!

These tricks will require lots of practice and won't be easy. They require a lot of patience, thought and courage. This is the sort of riding that will enable you to compete at competition level, and even with some of the big names. If you manage to master these moves, then you are at a high skill level and should be looking to develop your own tricks

Gyrator

The gyrator is a useful scuffing flatland trick. It can be done on either side of the bike, switch-footed, or used in complex sequences and combinations. The idea is to keep moving the bike around by scuffing the rear tire; aim for as many rotations as you can. You can hold the handlebars or the front pegs.

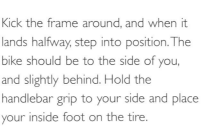

Ride along slowly and do a half lash maneuver to get into this. Stand on the peg switch-footed (your inside foot is on the front peg).

Kick the frame around, and when it lands halfway, step into position. The bike should be to the side of you, and slightly behind. Hold the handlebar grip to your side and place your inside foot on the tire.

Scuff the tire forward and use your free left arm for balance. If you feel your weight is too far forward, give the tire a couple of quick scuffs. If you feel like your weight is too far back, slow your scuffs down using your foot as a brake.

Scuff the tire to rotate the bike. It takes a lot of practice to control the direction of your bike, as the trick naturally moves in circles because of the slanted position. The bike moves in a clockwise direction if you are on the left side of the bike, and counter-clockwise direction if on the right.

You can still steer the bike by steering the tire in the direction you wish to go. When you are ready to pull out, put your scuffing foot back on to the pedal. Bring the bike forward.

Pass your handlebars back to your free hand and bring the bike in front of you to drop the front wheel back on to the floor. Place your other hand back on the grip, land your free foot back on the pedal and ride off.

Spinning lawnmower

This is one of the most fun tricks based on circular spins. This style of trick requires you to hold your body in to spin faster. Extend your body out to slow down. This varying body position technique is known as a turbine. It is the same principle as a spinning peg wheelie where you pull the bike closer to you to spin faster and you push the bike away from you to spin slower.

Start in a spinning wheelie position, with both hands on the handlebars. Lean back and pick the front wheel off the floor.

Carve in a circle, turning the handlebars 180 degrees at the same time as letting go of your outside grip. Use your free arm and leg to balance you; if you feel you are falling too far back, place your leg or your bike forward.

To move forward your balancing leg should be between your other leg and your bike, or you can move your bike forward by extending your arm. If you find that you are falling too far forward, extend your leg out backward or pull the bike in further toward you.

Once you are comfortable with your balance you can speed up the spin by pulling your free arm and free leg in closer to your body, and also pulling on the handlebars to bring the bike more upright.

When you finish this trick, lean slightly forward and at the same time turn the handlebars straight.

Place your hand back on the grip and your feet back on the pedals. When the wheels are straight, ride off.

Manual roll

The manual roll is the advanced version of the wheelie. The principle works in a similar way, but the balance is achieved purely from positioning your body rather than pedaling. This makes the maneuver trickier to master.

Roll at a comfortable speed. Lean backward, pull on the handlebars and straighten your legs to lift the front wheel off the floor.

Put your fingers on the rear brake lever, to cover the brake. If you feel like you are tipping over the back of the bike and about to fall off, pull the rear brake to drop the front wheel.

The important thing to remember for maintaining your balance is to look forward and give yourself a target distance to roll, lean back so your position is over the top of the rear wheel.

You can control the balance by bending your knees and making minor adjustments by leaning either to the left or to the right to keep in a straight line. It is important to keep your arms straight and your legs flexible.

Keep an equal amount of pressure on each pedal, sometimes it is an easy mistake to have more weight on the rear pedal, but the pressure on each pedal should be equal.

When you are ready, drop the front wheel on the floor by leaning forward or pulling the rear brake to return to normal riding position.

360 bunnyhop

In this advanced variation of the bunnyhop, you aim to rotate yourself and
the bike through a full rotation of 360 degrees. It follows the same
principle as the 180 bunnyhop (see page 64), but you continue around.
360s are popular tricks, and they cross all the BMX disciplines; flatland,
street, dirt and park.

Roll along at a steady speed, with
your feet on the pedals and your
hands on the grips. Before you start
to move, visualize you and the bike
completing a full rotation.

Get your weight to the back of the
bike, then compress your body by
bending your arms and knees.
Crouch down. Get ready to pull up
on the handlebars.

Start to carve in the direction you
want to spin. Pull up on the
handlebars as you spring up by
straightening your legs and arms. Turn
your body and look to the direction
you wish to turn.

As you rotate, look over your shoulder, continually turning into the direction of the rotation.

Continue to rotate, be aware of where you want to land. Until you have mastered this trick you may need to land the back wheel and complete the last part of the rotation on your back wheel.

Complete the trick by landing both wheels at the same time. While you practice, it is OK to land the rear wheel, followed by the front wheel. Make sure your wheels are straight before you ride off.

Full cab

This is a variation on the 360 degree bunnyhop, where you start from a fakie (rollback). It's similar to the forward version, and it can be done on a variety of different obstacles. The idea is to lift both wheels level during the jump.

To begin with start with a 180 endo or a 180 bunnyhop so you are rolling backward at a moderate speed.

Roll back, and compress your body. Wait until your pedals are level with the floor, then lock the rotation of your rear wheel using your foot on the pedal. As you lock the rear wheel the front wheel will start to lift.

Lift your body and turn your head to face the position you want to rotate. As the front wheel lifts off, pull the handlebars up and toward you. Lift your knees up into your body and turn into the direction you wish to spin.

When the bike reaches the 180 degree point, face the direction you are turning and keep the wheels level.

Rotate the bike for the last part of the rotation. Lift both wheels so they are parallel to the ground.

Land the bike as gently as possible. You should have enough speed to still be rolling backward, so you can either smoothie out of this or rockwalk out.

Bunnyhop barspin

In this trick you bunnyhop and spin the handlebars 360 degrees in mid-air. Before you attempt this trick you should be able to spin the handlebars 360 degrees on the floor comfortably. A bunnyhop barspin is a very quick trick, so you need to visualize the move before you start.

Ride quite slowly and compress your body ready to spring upward. Make sure that you have a strong grip on the handlebars.

Pull up on the handlebars to do a high bunnyhop. As this is a fast trick, you need to decide if you are going to spin the bars before you leave the floor, so visualize this now.

When in the air, pinch the seat with your knees to keep the bike stable. Try to make sure the bike is reasonably level and both wheels off the floor. Lift one hand.

TIP
Although both hands need to be on the
bike at the beginning and end of the
trick, choose one hand to be the
throwing hand and the other to catch.

Spin the handlebars in the direction you choose, as quickly as possible. Make sure your knees are out of the way from the spinning handlebars by keeping your legs straight.

It is important to try to keep your legs as straight and as far back as possible for bar clearance, but lean the top of your body slightly forward to avoid flipping off the back of the bicycle. Get ready to catch the bars.

As the handlebars spin around, catch them as they come around to 270 degrees. Grasp the handlebars with both hands, and land as gently as possible. Bend your knees slightly to absorb any impact.

Dumptruck

An advanced and useful scuffing flatland trick. A dumptruck can be done on either side of the bike, switch-footed or used in combinations of tricks.

Ride along slowly, with your left foot on the left peg. Pull up into a peg wheelie. Use your free leg to help maintain your balance.

Use your left hand to pull the handlebars up and use your right hand to grab either the front peg or fork leg.

Place the bike behind you, holding the peg or fork to your side and place your foot on the tire. There are quite a few different things happening simultaneously, but this should be performed as one fluid move.

Scuff the tire forward and use your left arm for balance. If you feel your weight is too far forward, give the tire a couple of quick scuffs.

If you feel like your weight is too far back, slow your scuffs down using your foot as a brake.

There is an instinctive urge to lean forward away from the bike, so it is a good idea to practice bringing the bike closer to you.

When you are ready to pull out, keep your foot on the tire and bring the bike forward. Pass the handlebars back to your free hand and bring the bike in front of you to drop the front wheel back on to the floor. Place your other hand back on the grip, land one foot back on the pedal and ride off.

Pinky squeaks

These continuous scuffing tailwhips, also known as "Pinky Whips," have a dynamic, rhythmic quality to them, and once you learnt the technique, you can do as many as you want, or maybe even throw in a variation.

Start with a fire hydrant maneuver, with your left foot on the front peg and with the bike frame rotating in a counter-clockwise direction.

As the frame comes round pull the front brake and step over the frame. The step over the frame is like a skip, with the leading foot stepping over slightly before the following foot.

Place your leading foot on the tire when the frame has passed, and place your following foot on the peg.

Give the tire one scuff and give your handlebars a clockwise rotational movement, to keep the momentum of the frame going, but take into account the shifting weight of the bike.

As the frame goes around again, repeat the same movements. There are lots of things happening at the same time in this trick, but the general movements should be rhythmic and repetitive. The amount of scuff you give the tire in unison with feathering the brakes is one of the ways you keep your balance.

You also need to alternate the pressure on the grip in relation to your foot repeatedly putting weight on the peg. When your left foot lands on the peg, apply extra pressure onto the right grip to counterbalance it. Catch the frame and place your feet back on the pedals when you have finished, before moving off.

Hang five

This is a classic rolling trick, beautiful in its simplicity and versatile enough to take to many different disciplines. Essentially, a hang five is a front wheel manual standing on the peg. It's a dangerous trick, so be ready to crash many times during practice.

Ride along at a speed you are comfortable with. Place your right foot on the front peg and push forward using both hands.

Scoop the peg back with your foot, and step forward off the pedal putting all of your weight onto the peg to lift the back wheel. Look forward to your destination.

Push forward until the bike seat reaches your rear. Use your free leg to balance you, swinging it back and forth like a pendulum. Continue to look in the direction you are going. Visualize achieving a certain amount of distance and focus on a destination mark.

Place your other foot on the peg too. When you are in the rolling position put a little more weight on your opposite hand to the foot standing on the peg (if your left foot is on the peg, put more weight on your right hand, if your right foot is on the peg put more weight on your left). Aim to do this trick in a straight line.

If you would like to steer this trick left or right, lean the handlebars to the side you wish to steer. If you want to steer to the left, place more weight on your left hand and lean to the left. Use a leg to balance you if you need to.

To exit the trick pull the handlebars backward, drop the back wheel on the floor and step back onto the pedal with your free foot. Then place your foot back on the pedal to complete.

Elbow glide

This maneuver is similar to a hang five but your body position is to the side of the bike instead of sitting on the seat. It can also be used as a way of getting into a hitchhiker trick. It is easy to get tangled up in the elbow glide, so please be at a very comfortable and confident level of riding before you attempt this trick.

Ride along with both hands on the handlebars. Place your outside foot on the front peg and your inside foot on the back peg, so you are standing on the side of the bike.

Lean forward, scoop the front peg backward to lift the back wheel, and let the rear end of the bike rise until the seat pushes up against the inside of your arm. The bike should now be locked into place.

Keep your head up and look in the direction you are going. Swing your balancing foot to move back and forth to maintain balance.

With the seat held in under your arm and close to your elbow, glide along the ground. You can use your free foot as a counterbalance, moving it up and down to maintain your position in the glide.

If you feel unstable, lean forward to adjust your balance. Continue using your free foot as an aid to your balance until you reach your pre-planned destination.

To pull out of the trick, pull back and let the back wheel drop to the floor gently. Place your balancing foot back on the peg, move your front foot back on the pedal, followed by your rear foot.

Karl cruiser

This is a similar rolling trick to the hang five, but because of its asymmetric positioning and its need for good upper body strength, it is also similar to side squeaks. It is a great trick to use for links, and you can also use it to set up tricks such as the hitchhiker. It is easy to get tangled up in the karl cruiser, so please be at a very comfortable and confident level with your riding before you attempt this trick.

Ride along with both hands on the handlebars. Place your outside foot on the front peg and your inside foot on the back peg, so you are standing on the side of the bike.

Lean forward, and scoop the front peg backward to lift the back wheel. Check your balance and get ready to lift your inside hand (the hand closest to the bike).

As the back wheel rises, grab the seat with your inside hand. The upper half of your body should lock, using your core strength. Initially this requires a bit of strength to hold.

TIP
It is useful to try to practice the
rolling part of this trick first. Try
pushing along the floor just to
get a feel for the move.

Keep your head up and look in the direction you are going. Swing your balancing foot to move back and forth to maintain your balance. If your foot is on the left peg, the trick should naturally carve to the right and vice versa.

Bring your inside leg in toward your body. This can help you to balance as you get ready to end the trick.

To pull the trick, let go of the seat, let the back wheel drop to the floor, and place your balancing foot back on peg. Move your front foot back on the pedal followed by your rear foot.

Whiplash

This is a rolling tail whip, where you bring the rear of the bike around. You can use your brake to feather the balance. It's a well-respected trick, especially when you start doing multiples of tricks in succession, and it has a huge list of difficult variations. When you have learned all the different stages of balance during the whiplash it should become one fluid move.

Roll along at a comfortable speed with your hands on grips, with your outside foot on the front peg and the other foot on the rear peg.

Kick the frame around with your rear foot. At the same time, move your handlebars in a circular motion; this will help the frame rotate around the bike. Use your free leg to balance. You may need to move your balance leg backward to stop yourself from falling over the handlebars.

When the bike has reached 180 degrees of its rotation, exchange your standing and balancing feet, place your balancing foot on the other peg, and now use your initial standing foot for balancing.

TIP

When the bike is in its rotation you can use your body as a balancing tool by leaning backward or forward over the handlebars. Make sure you don't lean too far forward initially in case you go over the handlebars.

The rear of the bike should continue to come round to complete its rotation. Continue to use your body and free leg for balance.

When the frame has completed just over 270 degrees of the rotation, aim to use your free balancing foot for catching the frame.

Place your foot back on the frame and move your foot from the front peg back onto the pedal and ride off.

Double-footed steamroller

This is a good trick to master to help you get a feel for double-footed rolling tricks. These are generally considered to be slightly harder than single-footed rolling tricks, as you need to use subtle keen bending movements to control your balance, rather than being able to use your whole leg. Try this first standing on both pegs.

Start off with a classic steamroller. Roll along at a comfortable speed with your hands on the grips, your inside foot on the rear peg and the outside foot on the front peg. Lean forward to lift the back wheel.

Kick the frame around. Move your handlebars in a circular motion to help spin the frame around. As the frame reaches the 180 degree position, grab hold of the seat.

Place your other foot on the other peg so both feet are in a symmetrical position on the pegs. Check that your wheels are aligned, and use your free arm for balance. Keep an equal amount of pressure on each peg. Hold the seat in front of you so there is a comfortable distance in front of you.

Pull back to a steamroller by taking one foot off a peg, and use your free leg for balance. Swing it back and forth like a pendulum.

When you wish to get back onto the bike, use your hand to bring the seat back round. Continue to control your balance as you align the wheels.

Drop the back wheel on the floor, drop the seat and aim to place your free balancing foot back on the frame. Then place both feet back on the pedals and ride off.

Hang nothing

This maneuver is essentially a no-footed hang five. You take both feet off the pegs and have all the weight on your handlebars and seat. It is good fun to do, but be prepared to bail at any time!

To get into this trick you ride into a regular hang five. Roll at a comfortable speed, place your foot onto the front peg and push into a hang five.

Begin to take the weight off the peg and put more weight on to your arms and seat. You can do this by leaning forward but be aware of your balance at all times.

When you feel comfortable take your foot off the peg completely and lean slightly further forward. Lock your arms and back using your core strength. Use your legs as balance, moving them back and forth. Keep the top part of your body locked and the bottom part relaxed and free.

Just as during a hang five, continue facing forward and look in the direction you are going. Try to visualize a target point, for example, five yards ahead of you. Aim to build this distance over time. If you need to, put your feet back on the pegs.

To pull out of the trick, swing your legs back onto the pedals. Lean back to return into a regular riding position, and keep your wheels aligned.

Allow the rear wheel to land gently on the ground, and check your body position before riding off.

Hang ten

This is a double-footed hang five. The hang ten takes its name from the surf trick where you place all ten toes over the front of the surf board. Make sure you are at a good level of confidence with hang fives before you even begin to think about attempting this trick.

Ride along at a moderate speed and get ready to place both feet on the front pegs in a hang position. As you get ready, find a good position for your cranks and pedals so you have maximum clearance. Aim to get the cranks off-vertical with the bottom pedal slightly forward.

Push yourself into a hang five. Place both feet on the pegs and grab hold of the seat behind you with the hand you feel most comfortable with.

Adjust your body position so you have a comfortable amount of space between the seat and the handlebars. Raise your hand from the handlebars; this is the hang ten position.

Move your arm back and forth to gain balance, and bend your knees back and forth to help your balance also. Check that you are facing forward into the direction that you are traveling, and try to keep your legs symmetrical with equal weight on both pegs.

When you are ready to exit the trick, place your balancing hand back on the grip. Adjust your body weight.

Drop the seat and allow the rear wheel to land gently on the ground. Step back on to the pedals.

Half-hiker

The half-hiker may be the little brother of the hitchhiker, but don't be fooled
— the rolling position of this maneuver is incredibly tricky for a couple of
reasons. It's asymmetric positioning (a bias weight to one side) makes it
difficult to find the balance point, and the close proximity of the bike
demands quick reactions for bailing.

Start with a comfortable speed, with
the cranks in a good position for
clearance (see previous trick). Your
pedals should be positioned so you
can clear them easily.

Get into a karl cruiser trick as you
roll, then place your free foot onto
the other peg. Let go of the
handlebars so you are rolling along
double-footed, holding onto the seat.

Bend your legs and use your free
arm to balance.

TIP

This is a scary balancing trick, and it is guaranteed you will fall forward, so be quick on your feet and be prepared to jump over your bike with lightning-fast cat-like reflexes while you practice.

Look up when you are rolling, keep your legs relaxed and like many double-footed rolling tricks, keep an equal amount of pressure on each peg.

Practice tipping the seat higher and lower to see what suits you. Tipping the seat higher makes the bike less heavy, but increases the difficulty of maintaining your balance.

To pull out of this trick, drop the rear wheel back on the floor, just like you would a karl cruiser.

Hitchhiker

This trick is possibly one of the hardest tricks to learn. It is named hitchhiker because you stand upright with the bike vertical with your free arm moving back and forth, as if hitching a lift. This is a classic flatland trick; if you can perform a hitchhiker you have definitely reached a certain level of flatland riding. Be prepared to put the work in to master this one; like with all good things it doesn't come easy.

To start a hitchhiker you can either do an elbow glide or a karl cruiser (a karl cruiser entry is shown here). Start with a comfortable speed. Do a half barspin so the handlebars are facing backward. This will give you more ground clearance when the trick is rolling.

Lift the rear wheel, and get into the karl cruiser position. Check that your weight is forward and you are feeing comfortably balanced.

Place your free foot onto the other peg and let go of the handlebars so you are rolling along double-footed, holding onto the seat. Push the bike forward so it starts to go in a vertical position. Move your hand from holding the seat to grabbing hold of the tire in one motion.

The hand goes from facing upward to facing downward to grab the top of the rear tire. As you grab the tire, push the bike forward. The wheel rotates round slightly and the hand ends up being at the back of the tire. The bike should be in front of you. Bend your knees and use your free hand to balance this trick.

When you are ready to pull out of this trick, you do the reverse of how you got into it. Pull the back wheel backward and place your hand back onto the seat.

Keep your weight forward as you pull the bike backward. When your hand catches the seat, take your foot off the inside peg, and aim to land it on the rear peg once the rear wheel has landed. Then move back onto the pedals to complete.

glossary

50 50—a grind or stall with both pegs on one side on an obstacle.

180—a 180 degree rotation usually performed as either a bunnyhop or jump.

360—a 360 degree rotation usually performed in the air.

Abubaca—a rear wheel stall on the edge of a ramp, or other obstacle.

Ad lugs—part of the frame to which you attach AD brakes.

Air—the action of rotating 180 degrees in the air off a ramp.

Amped—thrilled, excited.

Annodized—a technique of coloring metal.

Axle—the shaft on which the wheel revolves.

Backyard—scuffing trick on the back wheel.

Bail—to jump off the bike.

Bank—sloped area less than 90 degrees.

Bar ride—rolling along standing on the handlebars no handed.

Bead—the outside edge of the tire, which is stiffened by a wire.

Berm—an embankment on a track built up on the outside of a turn to create a banked curve.

Blender—spinning rolling trick.

Blunt—a rear wheel stall on the edge of a ramp, or other obstacle.

BMX—abbreviation for bicycle motocross.

Bottom bracket—the bearing that attaches the crankset to the frame and allows it to rotate freely.

Brake lever—a lever mounted on the handlebar used for activating the brake by pulling the cable.

Brake shoe—a rubber pad that stops the bike by pressing on the wheel rim, creating friction.

Bunnyhop—jumping the bike with both the front and rear wheels off the ground at the same time.

Bus—short for bus driver (see below).

Bus driver—bar-spin usually pushing the handlebars around.

Cables—used to connect the brake levers to the brakes.

Caboose—scuffing trick on the back wheel holding the fork or peg (also know as a dump truck).

Can-can—sticking your leg across the top of the frame, usually performed in a jump.

Candybar—sticking your leg over the handlebars, usually when in a jump.

Chain stays—part of the bicycle frame that runs parallel to the chain. It connects the bottom bracket to the rear dropouts.

Chain wheel—a one-piece front gear. The chain wheel is attached to the bottom bracket and crank.

Cherry picker—hopping trick with the bike upright.

Circle K—front wheel scuffing trick, standing on the front peg holding the seat and handlebars.

Cliff hanger—no handed front wheel roll sitting between the seat and the back wheel.

Coping—metal pipe on the edge of a ramp.

Crackpacker—double footed front wheel roll holding the seat.

Crooked—grind with front and rear opposing pegs on an obstacle.

Dab—to touch the floor gently with your foot when on the bike.

Death truck—a flatland trick that evolved from the dump truck which entails sitting on the headtube rolling on the rear peg with the bike vertical.

Deck—the flat top of a ramp, also known as a platform.

Disaster—air to 180 onto a ramp deck landing with rear half of the bike on the deck and front half on the transition.

Doubles—a set of two jumps.

Down tube—part of the bicycle frame, that slants downward at an angle. It runs from the head tube to the bottom bracket.

Downside—position of a bike in street or ramp riding, usually at a 90 degree angle instead of upright.

Drop-in—entering into a ramp from the top.

Drop out—the metal plates on the frame and forks where the wheels attach.

Fakie—going backward.

Fakie rock—a ramp trick with the top part of your bike on the deck of the ramp, bottom part on the ramp.

Feeble—a grind or stall with front wheel and rear peg on obstacle.

Foot jam—a front wheel stall using the foot as a brake.

Free wheel—a one-piece rear gear that allows the rider to back-pedal.

Fufanu—a rear wheel stall on the edge of an obstacle.

G-turn—a switch of direction in a sharp turn.

Grind—a trick where the peg or pedals grind along the edge/top of a wall, ledge rail or ramp.

Grips—plastic cover that goes on the handle bars at the end, to aid in gripping handle bars.

Gusset—a triangle of reinforcing steel located between the top and down tubes on your bike.

Gut lever—roll on the bike with body horizontal, with only your hands on the bike.

Gyro—a device that enables you to spin the handlebars a full 360 degrees without cable interference.

Halfpipe—a u-shaped ramp.

Head set—bearing set that attaches the forks to the frame and allows them to rotate.

Head tube—a short vertical tube at the very front, or head, of the bike. The front fork fits inside the head tube.

Hi-ten—High tensile steel usually used to make less expensive frames.

Hip—two adjoined inclines or transitions at an angle.

Holeshot—the lead out of the gate at the start of the race.

Hub—cylinder, that holds the axle of each wheel.

Hucker—someone who throws themselves at a trick with no fear or skill.

Hyperspastic—in fast circles.

Icepick—stall or grind position with just rear peg in contact.

Inside—the context of positioning yourself on the inside of a carve in flatland.

Kick flip—to kick the cranks into a 360 flip in mid air.

Knurled—a technique of texturizing metal to create a rough surface.

Lid—helmet.

Line—the path you take usually in a skatepark or trails.

Link—the joining together of two or more tricks.

Luc—a grind or stall with rear peg and pedal on an obsatcle.

Manual—the act of riding a wheelie without pedaling.

Nose manual—front wheel wheelie.

Nose pick—front wheel stall on an obstacle.

Nothing—a jump variation taking your hands and feet off in mid air.

Opposite—performing a trick.

Pegs-Platform—the flat surface on top of a ramp.

Platform pedals—the most commonly used pedals for trails, street and ramps. They have a platform that has little pegs that stick to your shoe.

Quarter—a curved ramp, one side of a halfpipe.

Rail—a hand rail grind.

Regular—the more familiar side of doing things (usually used in comparison to switch or opposite).

Rubber ride—rolling along standing upright on your grips.

Run—a sequential collection of tricks or links, usually associated with a contest.

Scuff—to move the tire along with your foot.

Seat post—the tube, which holds the seat and goes into the frame.

Seatstay—frame tubes in between the rear wheel and cranks.

Slam—a crash.

Slammed—a part pushed to the furthest point it can go.

Smith—a grind or stall with front peg and rear wheel on obstacle.

Spine—a ramp where two transitions meet at a point in the middle.

Sprocket—a profiled wheel with teeth that mesh into a chain, such as a chain wheel or rear cassette assembly.

Stall—the act of stalling, usually done on a ramp.

Stearer tube—the tube on top of forks which goes into the frame.

Step thru—a jump variation with leg kicked over the frame to the side.

Stoked—thrilled, excited.

Suicide—no handed jump variation clamping the seat with knees.

Superman—stretched no footed jump variation.

Switch—switch footed or opposite side.

Table—short for table top jump or air laying the bike flat.

Time Machine—flatland trick with bike vertical, spinning in circles on the rear wheel.

Tire tap—rear wheel stall on an obstacle.

Toboggan—a jump variation holding your seat with the handlebars at 90 degrees.

Toothpick—either a stall or grind position with just front peg contact.

Top tube—the top horizontal tube on a bicycle frame, between your head tube and seat tube.

Transition—a curved incline.

Tranny—short for transition.

Triples—a set of three jumps together.

Truckdriver—a 360 with a 360 barspin (sometimes called truck).

Tuck no hander—no handed jump variation resting the handlebars on your lap.

Turbine—spinning rolling trick.

Turndown—a jump variation turning the handlebars pointing downward with legs extended positioned to the side of the bike.

Vanderoll—forward roll on the floor, invented by Dave Vanderspeak.

Vert—halfpipe with vertical sides.

Whip—tailwhip bunny hop or jump.

X-up—turning your handlebars 180 degrees while still holding onto them and crossing your arms.

index

Acknowledgments

The publishers would like to thank Thomas Göring
and Timm Henger at KHE bikes (khebikes.com) for
their help with photographs and equipment.

A special thanks to Mario Carelse and
Oli Ward for their hard work performing
all the tricks for photography.